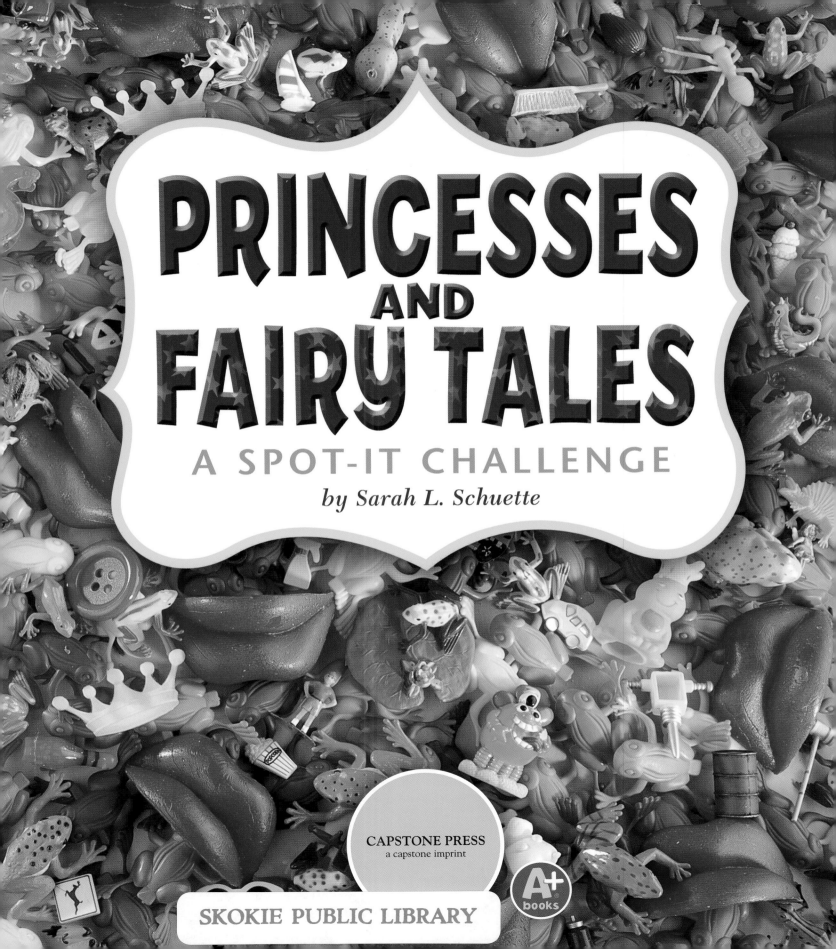

PRINCESSES
AND
FAIRY TALES

A SPOT-IT CHALLENGE

by Sarah L. Schuette

CAPSTONE PRESS
a capstone imprint

A+
books

A+ Books are published by Capstone Press,
1710 Roe Crest Drive, North Mankato, Minnesota 56003.
www.capstonepub.com

Library of Congress Cataloging-in-Publication Data
Schuette, Sarah L., 1976–
    Princesses and fairy tales: a spot-it challenge / by Sarah L. Schuette.
        p. cm—(A+ books.spot it)
    Includes bibliographical references.
    Summary: "Simple text invites the reader to find items hidden in fairy tale-themed
photographs"—Provided by publisher.
    ISBN 978-1-4296-5987-1 (library binding)
    1. Fairy tales. 2. Picture puzzles. I. Title.
    GR550.S345 2012
    398.2—dc23

                                                    2011017169

Credits
Jeni Wittrock, editor; Ted Williams, designer; Eric Manske, production specialist;
    Sarah Schuette, photo stylist; Marcy Morin, photo scheduler

Photo Credits
all photos by Capstone Studio/Karon Dubke

The author dedicates this book to her goddaughter, Muriel Hilgers.

Note to Parents, Teachers, and Librarians
Spot It is an interactive series that supports literacy development and reading enjoyment.
Readers utilize visual discrimination skills to find objects among fun-to-peruse, fairy tale-themed
photographs with busy backgrounds. Readers also build vocabulary through thematic groupings,
develop visual memory ability through repeated readings, and improve strategic and associative
thinking skills by experimenting with different visual search methods.

Printed in the United States of America in North Mankato, Minnesota.
112011   006456R

Table of Contents

Good Knight

Can you spot ...
- a helicopter?
- a horseshoe?
- a globe?
- a paintbrush?
- a raccoon family?
- a tree?

5

Potions

Can you spot ...

- a watermelon?
- a red crayon?
- a mouse trap?
- a teddy bear?
- an oar?
- a hammer?

Magic Shoes

Can you spot ...

- a sword?
- a tennis ball?
- a cockroach?
- a football?
- a reindeer?
- the letter "Q"?

Tea Party

Can you spot ...

- a zebra?
- a wrench?
- a ghost?
- a mouse?
- a sheep?
- an ant?

11

Fiery Lair

Can you spot ...
- the number "2"?
- a trumpet?
- a pinecone?
- an acorn?
- the letter "J"?
- a bone?

14

Camelot

Can you spot ...

- a toaster?
- a rose?
- two cherries?
- a pitchfork?
- a stingray?
- a lighthouse?

Unicorns

Can you spot ...

- toast with jam?
- a rocket ship?
- an ice skate?
- a traffic cone?
- three gifts?
- a sea star?

Rapunzel

Can you spot ...
- a sun?
- a trophy?
- a walrus?
- a pretzel?
- a tomato?
- a pig?

The Treasury

Can you spot ...

- a giraffe?
- a cat?
- a xylophone?
- a goose?
- a grill?
- two cupcakes?

Dress Up

Can you spot ...
- a hummingbird?
- a saxophone?
- a banana?
- a dragonfly?
- a life jacket?
- an ice skate?

23

Frog Kisses

Can you spot ...

- a purse?
- two shamrocks?
- a coffee pot?
- a crab?
- a spray bottle?
- a fighter jet?

Troll Bridge

Can you spot ...
- a birdhouse?
- a birthday candle?
- a castle?
- a skunk?
- a jug of milk?
- an ice cream treat?

Spot Even More!

Good Knight 4

Take another look to find a firefighter, a golf tee, a whistle, a genie's lamp, and a fire truck.

Potions 6

Try to find a piece of bread, the number "2", a record, a music note, a lantern, and a head of lettuce.

Magic Shoes 8

Check for a scuba mask, a tennis racket, a pencil sharpener, an eagle, and two tugboats.

Tea Party 10

See if you can spot a pat of butter, the letter "C", a crutch, a drum, and a koala.

Fiery Lair 12

Now look for a fishing vest, a honeybee, a skateboard, a chair, a scorpion, and a mousetrap.

Camelot 14

Try to find a broom, a sledgehammer, a witch, a scarecrow, a butterfly, and two palm trees.

Unicorns 16

See if you can spot two umbrellas, a bunch of grapes, a paperclip, and two bobbers.

Rapunzel 18

Try to find a bottle of sunscreen, a soda can, a clothes hanger, a lion, and a watering can.

The Treasury 20

This time find a donut, a cork, a pine tree, an ambulance, a pumpkin, and a monkey.

Dress Up 22

See if you can spot a raspberry, a cow, a yo-yo, two maple leaves, and one pair of underpants.

Frog Kisses 24

Now spot a pineapple, a pearl, a fish, a cowboy boot, a hotdog, and a robot.

Troll Bridge 26

Time to find a gingerbread man, a tiger, a ruler, a slice of pizza, a roller skate, and a sprig of mistletoe.

Extreme Spot-It Challenge

Just can't get enough fairy tale fun? Here's an extra challenge. Try to spot:

- a motorcycle helmet
- a dragon
- a cabbage
- a UFO
- a donkey
- a ladybug
- the Statue of Liberty
- a hamburger
- a turtle
- a lop-eared rabbit
- the letter "B"
- a fishing pole
- a Christmas stocking
- a pot of sunflowers
- a cooked turkey
- a vampire bat

Read More

Chedru, Delphine. *Spot It Again!: Find More Hidden Creatures.* New York: Abrams Books for Young Readers, 2011.

Marks, Jennifer L. *Fun and Games: A Spot-it Challenge.* Spot It. Mankato, Minn.: Capstone Press, 2009.

Schuette, Sarah L. *Halloween Hunt: A Spot-it Challenge.* Spot It. Mankato, Minn.: Capstone Press, 2011.

Internet Sites

FactHound offers a safe, fun way to find Internet sites related to this book. All of the sites on FactHound have been researched by our staff.

Here's all you do:

Visit *www.facthound.com*

Type in this code: **9781429659871**

 **Super-cool stuff!** Check out projects, games and lots more at **www.capstonekids.com**